CAMBRIDGE ENGLISH QUALIFICATIONS

Practice Tests
A1 Movers

• PETRINA CLIFF •

Four practice tests

OXFORD

UNIVERSITY PRESS

OXFORD
UNIVERSITY PRESS

Great Clarendon Street, Oxford, OX2 6DP, United Kingdom

Oxford University Press is a department of the University of Oxford.
It furthers the University's objective of excellence in research, scholarship,
and education by publishing worldwide. Oxford is a registered trade
mark of Oxford University Press in the UK and in certain other countries

© Oxford University Press 2018

The moral rights of the author have been asserted

First published in 2018

2022 2021 2020 2019

10 9 8 7 6 5

No unauthorized photocopying

Links to third party websites are provided by Oxford in good faith and for
information only. Oxford disclaims any responsibility for the materials
contained in any third party website referenced in this work

ISBN: 978 0 19 404263 5   Cambridge English Qualifications A1 Movers
Practice Tests Pack

ISBN: 978 0 19 404264 2   Cambridge English Qualifications A1 Movers
Practice Tests Student Book

ISBN: 978 0 19 404266 6   Cambridge English Qualifications A1 Movers
Practice Tests Audio access card

ISBN: 978 0 19 404265 9   Cambridge English Qualifications Practice Tests
Audio

Printed in China

This book is printed on paper from certified and well-managed sources

ACKNOWLEDGEMENTS

Back cover photograph: Oxford University Press building/David Fisher

Illustrations by:

Cover by Peter Stevenson/Linden Artists

Peter Stevenson Linden Artists pp.title page, 17, 39, 61, 83

Simon Smith pp.6, 21, 28, 32, 39, 50, 54, 72, 83

Michael Garton/Bright Agency pp.9, 10, 54, 65, 71, 87

IFA Design Ltd. (main illustrator Steve Evans) pp.4, 5, 7–9, 12, 14, 18–20,
22–27, 29–49, 51–53, 58, 61–64, 66–70, 73–86, 88–90

Contents

Part 1

- 5 questions -

Listen and draw lines. There is one example.

Ann   Jane   Daisy   Paul

Jill   Sam   Kim

Part 2

- 5 questions -

Listen and write. There is one example.

Sports For All!
Every Day After Class!

Name: Tom Baker

Age: ....9...........

1 Favourite Sport: ....

Class: ....5H.........

2 Teacher: Mr. ....

Address: 3 High Street

3 Green ....

✂ -

4 Things to bring: ....

water

sweater

5 ....

Part 3

- 5 questions -

Lily did some homework for her teacher about the places her family and friends like. Which places do Lily's family and friends like?

Listen and write a letter in each box. There is one example.

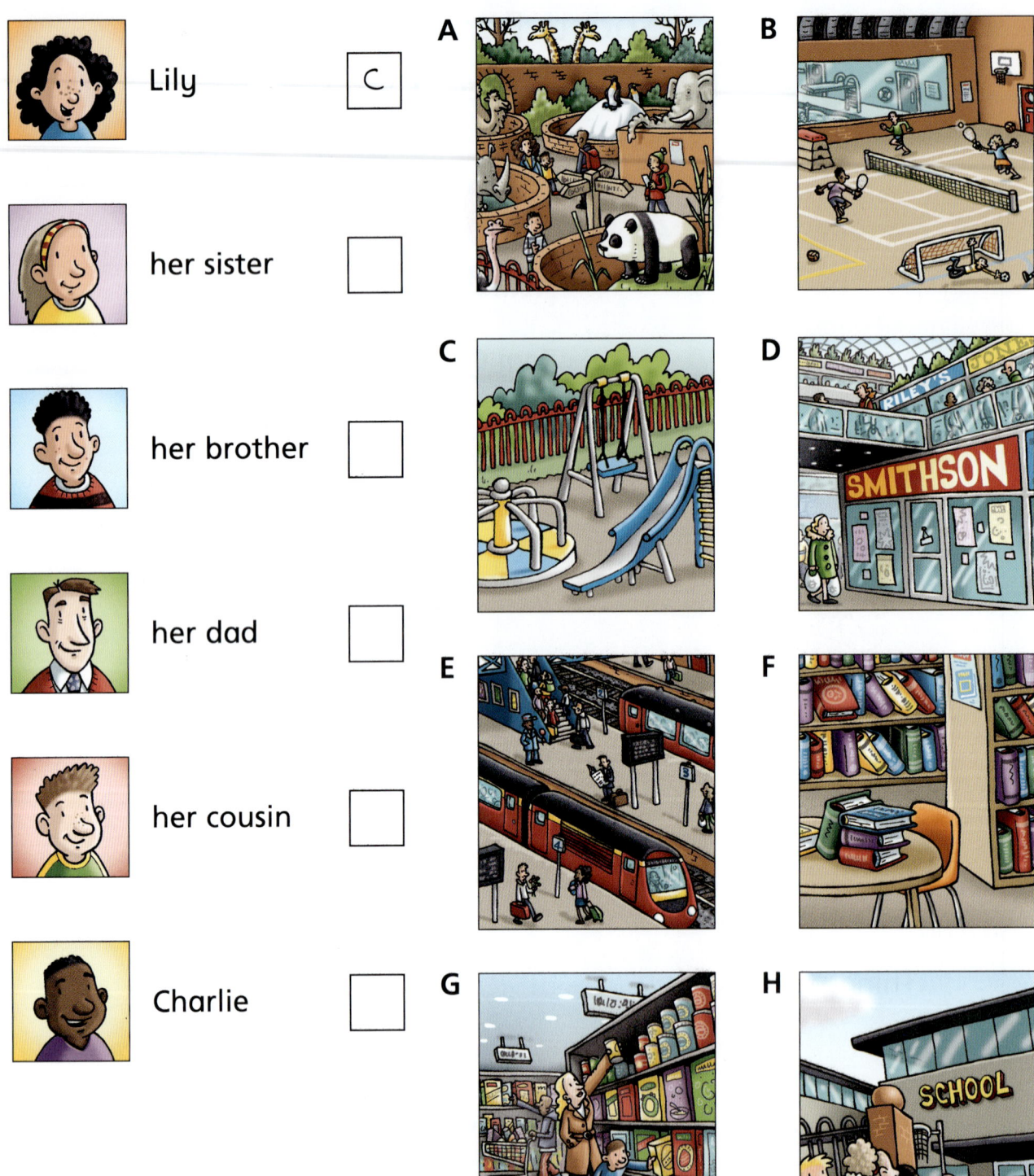

Part 4

- 5 questions -

Listen and tick (✔) the box. There is one example.

Which is Daisy's sister?

A ✔   B ☐   C ☐

1   How does Jack go to school?

A ☐   B ☐   C ☐

2   What did Sally do at the weekend?

A ☐   B ☐   C ☐

3 Which book does Mary want to find?

A

B

C

4 What can Peter see from his window?

A

B

C

5 Where does Jane want to go?

A

B

C

Part 5

Listen and colour and write. There is one example.

The

The

Reading & Writing

Part 1

- 5 questions -

Look and read. Choose the correct words and write them on the lines. There is one example.

the moon

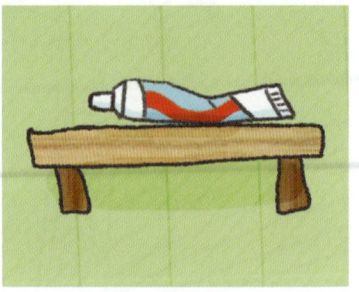

toothpaste

a bowl

penguins

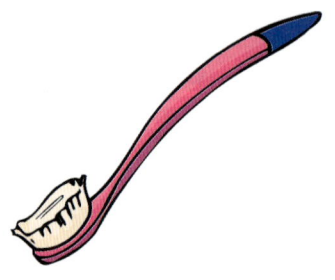

toothbrush

snails

a bottle

stars

Example

You can put water or juice in this. ....a bottle...........

Questions

1   You see these above you in the sky at night. ....

2   You can have soup or fruit in this. ....

3   These animals live in cold places on the ice and they eat fish. ....

4   When you want to clean your teeth, you put this on a toothbrush. ....

5   These animals move very slowly, they have shells on their backs and they eat leaves. ....

Part 2

Read the text and choose the best answer. There is one example.

Example

Julia: Are those new shoes Clare?

Clare: A   Yes, they do.
          B   Yes, they are.
          C   Yes, they're shoes.

Questions

1   Julia: Where did you find them?

    Clare: A   Yes, in town.
              B   Last week.
              C   In a shop in town.

2 Julia: Was it a good shop?

   Clare: A Yes, well.
           B Yes, very.
           C Yes, good.

3 Julia: Do you go shopping a lot?

   Clare: A Every weekend!
           B All weekends!
           C Last weekend!

4 Julia: And what do you buy?

   Clare: A I like buying clothes.
           B I'd like to buy clothes.
           C I liked buying clothes.

5 Julia: Would you like to go shopping this weekend?

   Clare: A I like to.
           B I'd love to.
           C I'd want to.

6 Julia: Where shall I see you?

   Clare: A At the station.
           B On the station.
           C To the station.

Part 3

- 6 questions -

Read the story. Choose a word from the box. Write the correct word next to numbers 1–5. There is one example.

Last week our class went to a farm in the ....countryside.... . It was

a beautiful (1) .... day and everyone talked and

(2) .... on the bus.

When we got there, we saw lots of chickens in a field near the farm

house. Our first job was to feed them. Then the farmer took us around

the farm. He had a dog called Sam. Sam was so clever. He looked

for the sheep and found lots! My classmates had a ride on a really

(3) .... horse, but I didn't. It was too dangerous!

In the afternoon we went around the fields on a huge tractor! The

farmer grows (4) .... and sells them at the market, so we all

helped him to water them. It was a brilliant day!

Today at school our teacher told us to (5) .... stories about

our day on the farm. This is mine.

Example

countryside	pencils	farmer
write	big	swim
laughed	vegetables	sunny

(6) Now choose the best name for the story.

Tick one box.

The farmer's day ☐

How animals live ☐

Going to the farm ☐

Part 4

- 5 questions -

Read the text. Choose the right words and write them on the lines.

The Library

Example One of the best buildings in town to go to ....on.......... a wet day is the library.

1 When you want to know .... about the world you live in, there are lots of books to read. Books can teach you many things too: how to build model trains, or how to fix your bike.

Many people think that reading real books is better than

2 reading e-books, and you can .... books home with you. The library is a great place to do your homework

3 .... you can use the computers. It's also quiet,

4 so try .... to talk loudly when you are there. Some libraries have a shop where you can buy things

5 .... pens and maps.

Example	on	in	at
1	something	nothing	sometimes
2	take	took	taking
3	so	or	because
4	not	no	now
5	like	of	on

Part 5

- 7 questions -

Look at the pictures and read the story. Write some words to complete the sentences about the story. You can use 1, 2 or 3 words.

Jim's birthday

My name's Jim and yesterday it was my birthday. I was nine and I got lots of nice presents from my family. Mum took pictures when I opened them. From Mum and Dad, I got a red bike. It's new and better than my old one. They also got me a helmet. Mum says I have to wear that when I go riding. And my grandparents bought me a laptop. I love it!

Examples

It was Jim's ......birthday...... yesterday.

His family got him some ......presents...... .

Questions

1   Jim's parents bought him a .... and a new bike.

2   He also got .... from his grandparents.

So after school I went to the swimming pool with three friends. When we got there we didn't want to swim at first because the water was very cold, but when we did we had great fun. Then Mum shouted, 'Time to go home!' so we had a shower and got dressed quickly.

3   After school Tom went to the swimming pool with ....

4   At first the water was cold so they .... to swim.

5   When they got out of the pool they went for a .... before they got dressed.

When we got home, we played board games in my bedroom. Then Mum called us and we went into the kitchen and had pancakes and strawberry milkshakes. Then at nine o'clock, my friends all said goodbye. It was a great birthday, but next year I really want a huge party because I'd like to invite all the kids in my class!

6 After playing board games, Jim and his friends ate some

....

7 For his next birthday, Jim would like to have .... with his classmates.

Part 6

- 6 questions -

Look and read and write.

Examples

    The boy is playing with a toy   ....car............

    How many dogs are there?   ....three............

Complete the sentences.

1   The girl who's playing with a boat
    is standing in the   ....

2   The girl with the purple coat is holding a   ....

Answer the questions.

3   Where is the cat?   ....

4   What colour are the leaves?   ....

Now write two sentences about the picture.

5   ....

6   ....

22

Picture Story: The Rabbit and the Treasure

Pirates

Find the Different Ones

Part 1

- 5 questions -

Listen and draw lines. There is one example.

Lucy   Daisy   Fred   Sally

Peter   Tom   Jane

Part 2

- 5 questions -

Listen and write. There is one example.

Play World Funfair

	Your age:	.........eleven.........
1	Day you came:	....
2	Favourite ride:	.... boat

Café

	Did you go?	..........yes..........
3	What did you eat?	....
4	Name of your teacher:	Mr. ....
5	Time you left park:	....

Thank you for helping us. We hope you come to Play World Funfair again soon!

Part 3

- 5 questions -

Zoe is telling her teacher about the different people in her family. What does each person in Zoe's family do at the weekend?

Listen and write a letter in each box. There is one example.

Part 4

- 5 questions -

Listen and tick (✔) the box. There is one example.

Which is Vicky's teacher?

 A ☐

 B ☐

 C ✔

1   What hasn't Jim got with him?

 A ☐

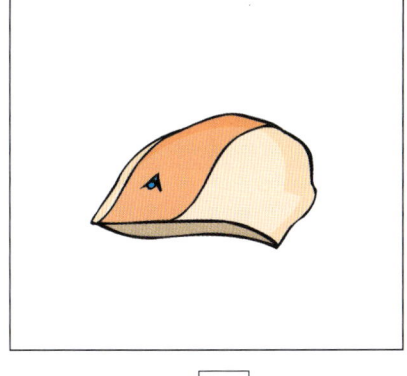 B ☐

 C ☐

2   Where's the station?

 A ☐

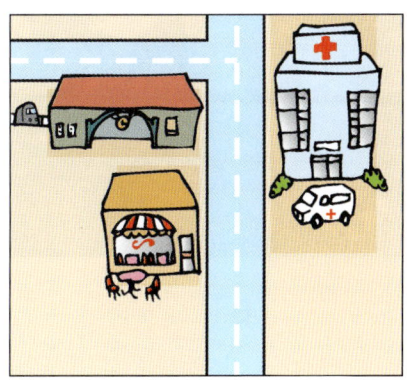 B ☐

 C ☐

3   What did Jack do last night?

A ☐   B ☐   C ☐

4   Which is Sue's homework?

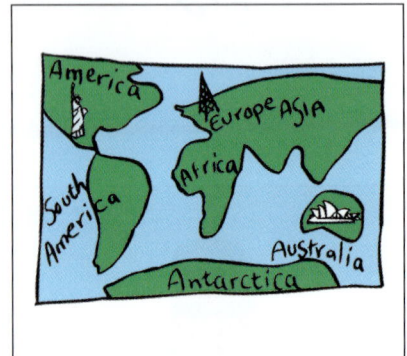 

A ☐   B ☐   C ☐

5   Which is Nick's book?

A ☐   B ☐   C ☐

Part 5

- 5 questions -

Listen and colour and write. There is one example.

Reading & Writing

Part 1

- 5 questions -

Look and read. Choose the correct words and write them on the lines. There is one example.

clouds

a hospital

ice cream

a rainbow

a library

pancakes

a doctor

a temperature

Example

You go here when you feel ill. ....hospital...........

Questions

1 When people get sick and feel very hot, they have this. Then they go and see the doctor. ....

2 You eat these after your dinner. They're very nice with sauce on them. ....

3 You see this after the rain, when the sun comes out and everything is still wet. ....

4 You can read books here or take them home to read. ....

5 These can be grey or white. Rain comes from them. ....

Part 2

- 6 questions -

Read the text and choose the best answer. There is one example.

Example

Fred: Do you play football Jim?

Jim: A   Yes, I like
    B   Yes, I do.
    C   Yes, please.

Questions

1   Fred: Where do you play?

    Jim: A   At the sports centre.
        B   To the sports centre.
        C   On the sports centre.

2 Fred: Can I come and watch you?

   Jim: A   Yes, I like that.

             B   Yes, I liked that.

             C   Yes, I'd like that.

3 Fred: I've got some tickets for the game on Saturday.

   Jim: A   Yes you have!

             B   Wow that's great!

             C   You get them!

4 Fred: Do you want to come with me?

   Jim: A   I'm sorry I can't.

             B   I'm sorry I didn't.

             C   I'm sorry I haven't.

5 Fred: Oh dear! Why not?

   Jim: A   I could go out with my family.

             B   I've got to go out with my family.

             C   I went out with my family.

6 Fred: Have a good day then!

   Jim: A   OK. Us too!

             B   OK. Me too!

             C   OK. You too!

Part 3

- 6 questions -

Read the story. Choose a word from the box. Write the correct word next to numbers 1–5. There is one example.

Last year I went to a beautiful place with my family. Dad took us in

the car. There were waterfalls and a huge ....Lake......... too. There

weren't any boats on the lake, because it was very (1) ....

that day.

People were ice skating, so my sister and I put on our hats,

(2) .... , coats and ice skates. Then we tried to skate.

When we started we weren't very good and we went slowly and

carefully. Then we got better and we skated around with the other

people. It was really exciting and we enjoyed it a lot! Dad had a new

(3) .... and he took lots of great pictures.

At about 6 o'clock, we left the lake and drove along a mountain road

to a café in a little (4) .... We were very hungry and we

all (5) .... noodles with tomato sauce on them. The food

was great! After that we were tired so Dad took us home and we went

straight to bed!

Example

lake	photos	map
camera	scarves	hid
village	ate	cold

(6) Now choose the best name for the story.

Tick one box.

Winter sports are easy! ☐

A great day with my family ☐

A quiet afternoon by the lake ☐

Part 4

- 5 questions -

Read the text. Choose the right words and write them on the lines.

Animal Families

Example There ....are.......... different kinds of animals and we

can put these animals into families. There are birds which

come from eggs and can fly. And some animals, like snails,

1 have bodies with shells on .... backs.

Different animals like different food. A lion likes meat, a

2 panda loves plants and leaves and a monkey ....

fruit and vegetables. And they live in different places: bears

like the mountains, tigers and snakes live in the jungle.

3 Then there are lizards and frogs .... live in lakes

4 and rivers when they are young, ... come out

5 of the water when they are .... And there are

fish that live all the time under the waves in the sea.

Example	is	are	were
1	our	his	their
2	eats	eat	ate
3	which	what	when
4	because	but	or
5	oldest	younger	older

Part 5

Look at the pictures and read the story. Write some words to complete the sentences about the story. You can use 1, 2 or 3 words.

Lost in the forest

Hello. I'm Charlie. Last week I went for a picnic with Mum and Dad, my older brother, Paul, and my dog, Bouncer. At one o'clock everyone was hungry. Dad stopped in a car park near a field and Mum put a blanket on the grass. Then we carried the food and drink from the car. We had chicken and cheese sandwiches and milkshakes, too. Bouncer ate sausages – his favourite food. Then Mum and Dad started to read their books and Bouncer went to sleep. It was all very boring and we wanted to do something exciting.

Examples

Charlie had a ...._picnic_........ with his family last week.

The family had a picnic lunch in a field, which had a ......_car park_...... next to it.

Questions

1   The family ate sandwiches and drank ....

2   After the picnic, Charlie's dog .... to sleep.

Paul and I got a map from the car and found there was a forest near where we were. We thought it would be nice to go for a walk there. Then Paul said, 'I don't know where we are'. We looked at the map carefully but it was difficult to read and we didn't know how to go back to Mum and Dad. Paul was frightened and I was too. We shouted and shouted but we couldn't see any people! We tried to be brave and we sat under some trees and waited. But it was terrible!

3   The children wanted to have …..................…… in the forest.

4   The children couldn't read their map and were …..................…….. because they didn't know how to find their parents.

5   They …..................……. in the forest for their parents to come.

Then Bouncer found us, and he knew how to go back to Mum and Dad. He went first and showed us where they were. Clever dog! Mum and Dad were very happy when they saw us again. They took us to a really nice café. Paul had a burger and I had a huge pancake. Paul and I don't go for walks in the forest now. We think it's too dangerous!

6   After Bouncer found the children, the family went to

.... and had something to eat.

7   Charlie ate ....

Part 6

Look and read and write.

Examples

The girl has got curly   ....hair.........

What colour is the cat that's inside the café?   ....black.........

Complete the sentences.

1   There is a clock above the   ....

2   There are three cakes on the biggest   ....

Answer the questions.

3   How many children are there in the café?   ....

4   What is the little boy doing?   ....

Now write two sentences about the picture.

5   ....

6   ....

Picture Story: Daisy helps her mum

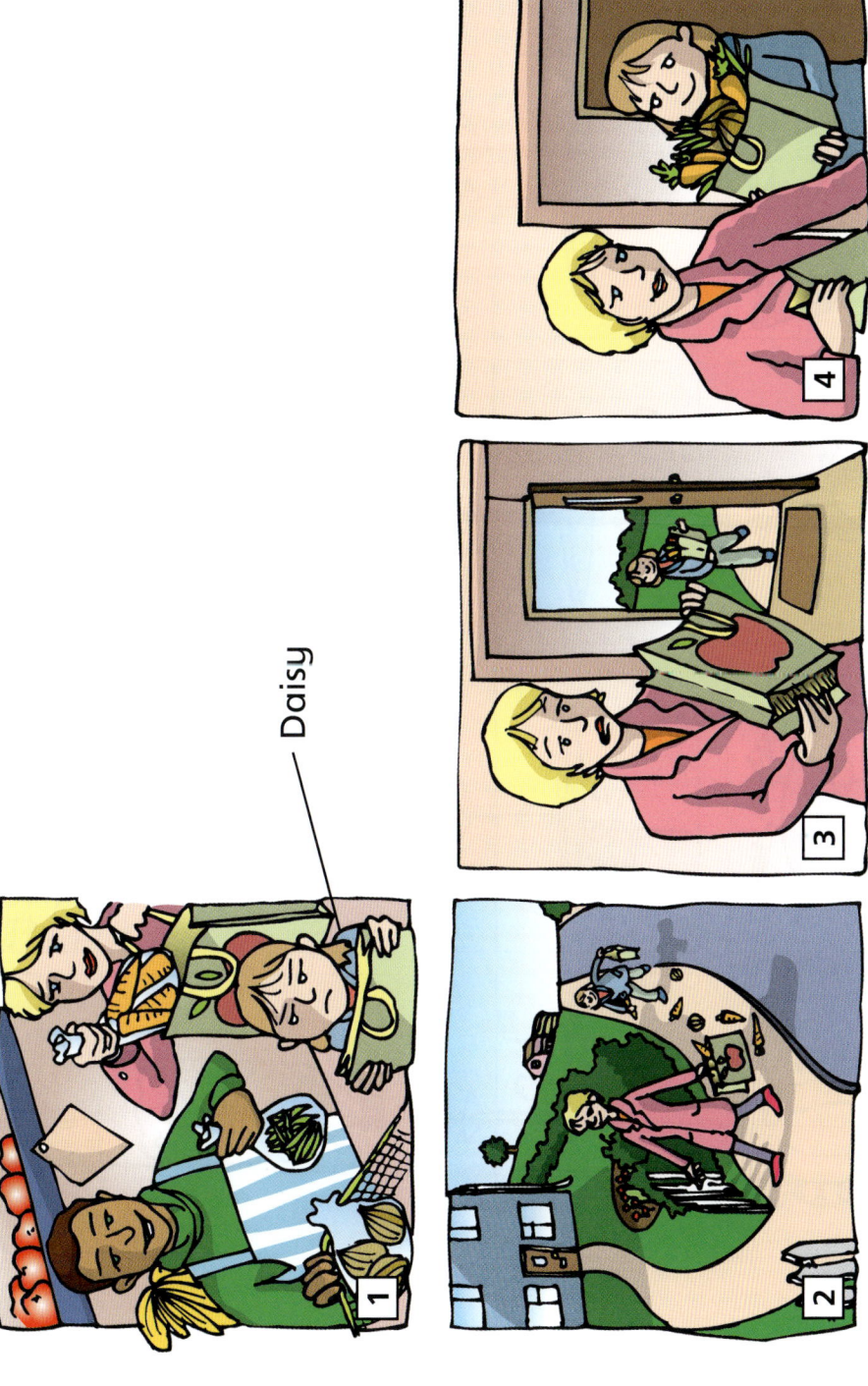

Daisy

46

Part 1

- 5 questions -

Listen and draw lines. There is one example.

Tony   Vicky   Tom   John

Anna   Bill   Kim

Part 2

- 5 questions -

Listen and write. There is one example.

New Start Sports Centre
Party Time!

Kind of party: ....games........ in sports hall

1 Name of parent: Mrs. ....

2 Day of party: .... at 4 pm

3 Number of children coming: ....

4 Food: .... and chips

5 Drink: ....

Part 3

- 5 questions -

Jack is telling his mother about the school trip he went on and about what everybody enjoyed doing. What did everybody enjoy doing on the school trip?

Listen and write a letter in each box. There is one example.

Part 4

- 5 questions -

Listen and tick (✔) the box. There is one example.

Which is Bill's uncle?

 **A** ☐

 **B** ☐

 **C** ✔

---

1   Which is Sally's baby cousin?

 **A** ☐

 **B** ☐

 **C** ☐

2   What's Fred doing after school?

 **A** ☐

 **B** ☐

 **C** ☐

3   What did Paul do in the holidays?

A ☐   B ☐   C ☐

4   Which clowns did Anna see?

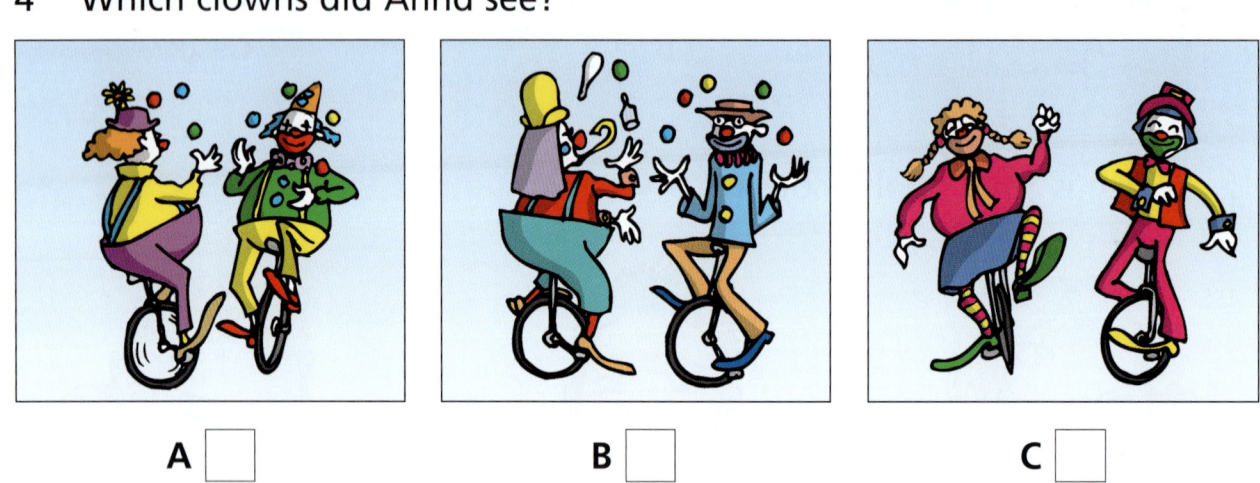

A ☐   B ☐   C ☐

5   Where's Jim's DVD game?

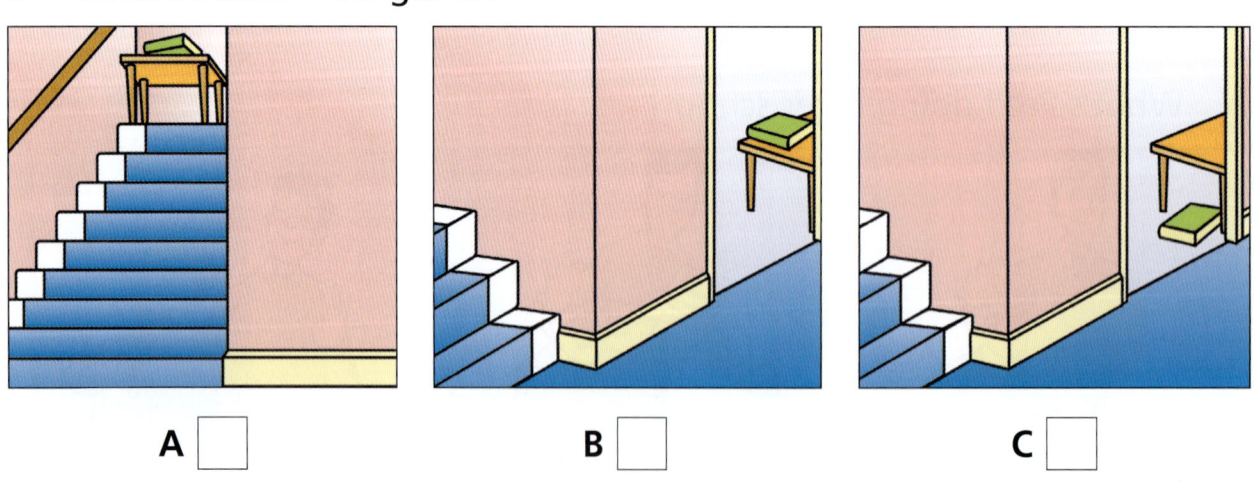

A ☐   B ☐   C ☐

Part 5

- 5 questions -

Listen and colour and write. There is one example.

By the

By the

Reading & Writing

Part 1

- 5 questions -

**Look and read. Choose the correct words and write them on the lines.
There is one example.**

a circus

a cough

a building

a cook

earache

a dentist

a funfair

stomach-ache

Example

You can get this when you listen
to loud music.   ....earache............

Questions

1   You go and see this person if you   ....
    have a problem with your teeth.

2   You have this after eating too many   ....
    cakes, sweets or chocolates.

3   You can see clowns and people who   ....
    do really cool things here.

4   People live or work in one of these places.   ....
    They can sometimes be very tall.

5   This is the person who works in a restaurant ....
    and makes meals in the kitchen there.

Part 2

- 6 questions -

Read the text and choose the best answer. There is one example.

Example

Jane: Mum! Where are you?

Mum: A   To your bedroom.
         B   In your bedroom.
         C   At your bedroom.

Questions

1   Jane: What are you doing?

    Mum: A   I paint.
             B   I'm painting.
             C   I painted.

2   Jane: Oh, the cupboard looks nice. When did you start?

Mum: A   This morning.
        B   That morning.
        C   The morning.

3   Jane: Can I help you?

Mum: A   Yes, you do.
        B   Yes, you can.
        C   Yes, you help.

4   Jane: Shall I paint the walls?

Mum: A   No, don't go there.
        B   No, don't tell me.
        C   No, don't do that.

5   Jane: Why not?

Mum: A   I like cleaning them first.
        B   I cleaned them first.
        C   I'd like to clean them first.

6   Jane: OK. Shall I get some water then?

Mum: A   Yes, thank you.
        B   Yes, you do.
        C   Yes, I want.

Part 3

- 6 questions -

Read the story. Choose a word from the box. Write the correct word next to numbers 1–5. There is one example.

Last week my favourite cousin came to our ....house........ . His

name's Peter. He's got a big motorbike and one afternoon he said 'Come

for a ride with me, Nick!'

We put on jeans, scarves, black **(1)** .... and helmets. Then

Peter and I looked at the map and off we went. It was a

(2) .... day and Peter went quickly. I held on to him and

we rode along a little road that went up into the mountains. It was

very exciting.

Then we were at the top. We put the motorbike under a tree and sat

down on the grass to eat our picnic. We had **(3)** .... ,

lemonade and oranges. Peter **(4)** .... to some goats below

us. They looked very **(5)** ....down there at the bottom of

the mountain. Then Peter said, 'It's seven o'clock!' We jumped on the

motorbike and went home.

Example

house	listened	jackets
pointed	windy	glass
blanket	sandwiches	small

(6) Now choose the best name for the story.

Tick one box.

A windy day ☐

Climbing in the mountains ☐

An exciting afternoon ☐

Part 4

- 5 questions -

Read the text. Choose the right words and write them on the lines.

How to take a good photograph

Example Children of all ages ....Love.......... cameras. It's easy to

pick one up and take a picture.

1 But you want to take a good picture. .... do

you do? Point your camera carefully before you take the

picture. For example, when you are taking a picture of your

2 sister, ... you see the top of her head? Is

3 .... a huge building behind her? Do you want it

4 in your picture? Asking .... questions helps you

to take a good photograph.

And you must think about the weather. A sunny day is best.

5 But .... is the sun? For the best pictures the sun

must be behind you.

Example	loving	love	loved
1	Why	How	What
2	can	want	did
3	it	this	there
4	this	that	these
5	where	when	which

Part 5

- 7 questions -

Look at the pictures and read the story. Write some words to complete the sentences about the story. You can use 1, 2 or 3 words.

Friends go to the cinema

My name's Mary and my best friend is Vicky. Last Saturday Vicky phoned me and said, 'Shall we go and see a film?' I said, 'But my favourite pop star is singing in town. I thought we said we'd go and see him.' But Vicky told me she couldn't get tickets. I said, 'OK, let's go to the cinema, then.' I told her I'd meet her at the cinema at two o'clock, in front of the building.

Examples

Mary's friend Vicky ....phoned........ her last Saturday.

Vicky asked Mary to go and see a ....film......... with her.

Questions

1   Mary wanted to see a .... she really likes but there weren't any tickets.

2   Mary said she would meet Vicky at .... outside the cinema.

There were a lot of people outside the cinema. I looked for Vicky but I couldn't see her there. I went into the cinema, bought an ice cream then went and sat down. Then the film started. I loved it because there were two really famous film stars in the film – that was so cool! But I was sad that Vicky wasn't with me.

3   Mary waited outside the cinema but she .... her friend.

4   Before Mary found a place to sit in the cinema, she .... something to eat.

5   Mary enjoyed the film because there were some .... people in it.

After the film, the first person I saw was Vicky! I said, 'Where were you?' and she answered, 'I came after the film started so I sat behind you.' Then we went to a café and had milkshakes. We talked about the film and then Mum came to take us home. 'Shall we go and see another film next week?' Vicky asked me. 'OK,' I said, 'but you must sit with me!' Vicky laughed.

6   Mary didn't see Vicky in the cinema because Vicky .... her.

7   In the café, Vicky and Mary had some ....

Part 6

- 6 questions -

Look and read and write.

Examples

The girls who are in the water are ....swimming......

What has the man in the shop got? ......ice creams.....

Complete the sentences.

1   The boy who's on the stairs is wearing a red ....

2   The girl in the red swimsuit is standing under a ....

Answer the questions.

3   How many children are in the boat? ....

4   What is the girl with the baseball cap holding? ....

Now write two sentences about the picture.

5   ....

6   ....

Picture Story : The Night Monster

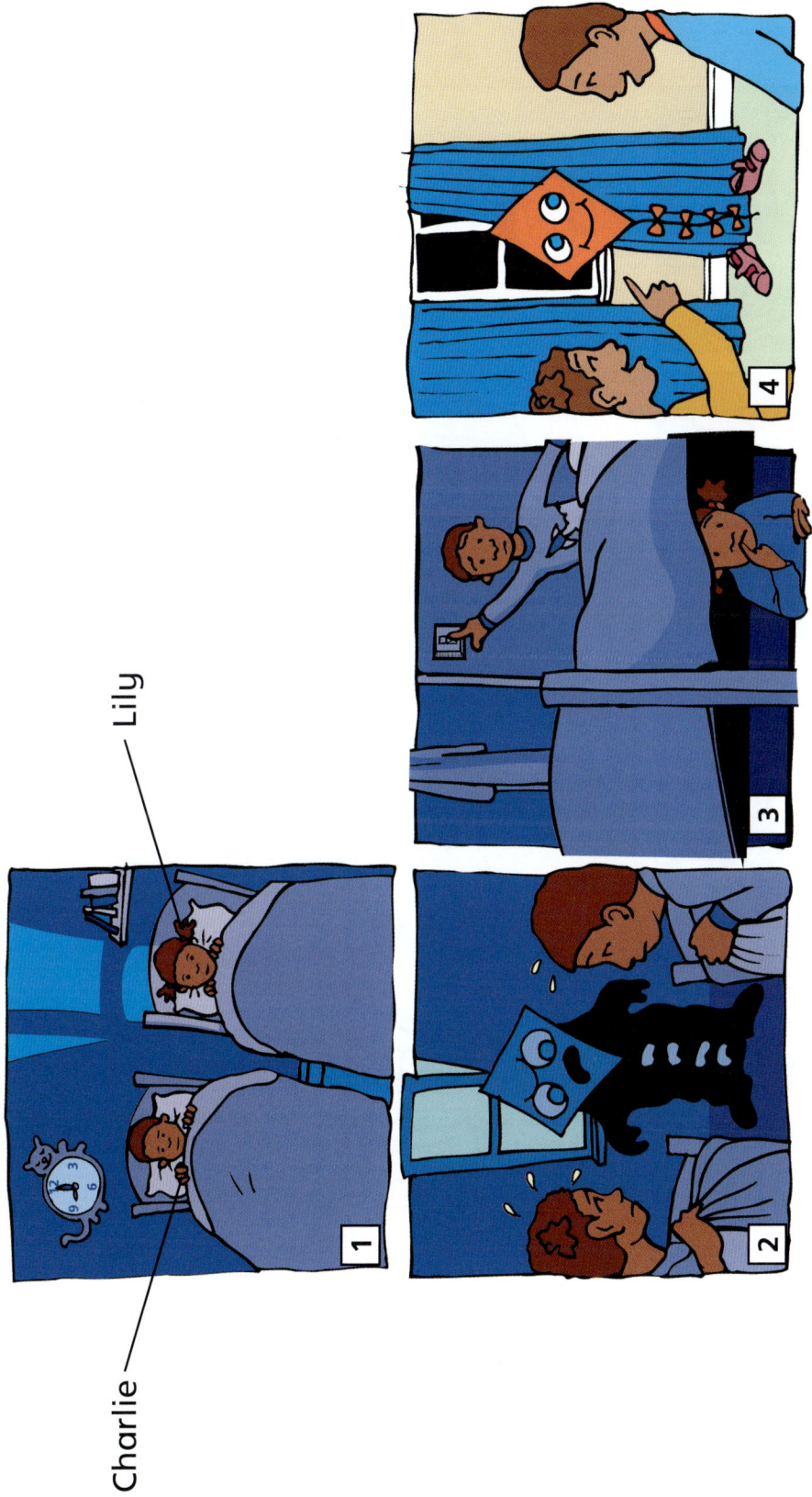

Charlie

Lily

Part 1

- 5 questions -

Listen and draw lines. There is one example.

Sally   Paul   Mary   Tom

Alex   May   Lucy

Part 2

- 5 questions -

Listen and write. There is one example.

Homework

Write an English ....story.........

1 Number of words: ....

Story about: a good party or

2   favourite ....

3 Give homework to
   teacher after the: ....

4 Teacher's name: Mr. ....

5 Learn about .... for test

Part 3

- 5 questions -

Sally is talking to her uncle about the things her family bought when they were on their holidays. What did Sally and her family buy when they were on their holidays?

Listen and write a letter in each box. There is one example.

Part 4

- 5 questions -

Listen and tick (✔) the box. There is one example.

Which animals did Kim see at the zoo?

A ✔   B ☐   C ☐

1   Which cake did Lucy buy for her Dad?

A ☐   B ☐   C ☐

2   Which boy is Alex?

A ☐   B ☐   C ☐

3 What did Ben wear for the party?

A

B

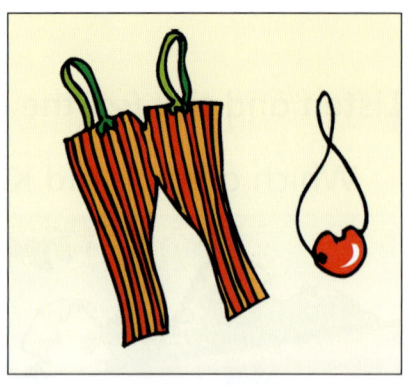

C

4 What did Fred see in the park?

A

B

C

5 What's Mary doing?

A

B

C

Part 5

- 5 questions -

Listen and colour and write. There is one example.

Reading & Writing

Part 1
- 5 questions -

Look and read. Choose the correct words and write them on the lines. There is one example.

salad

a balcony

stairs

fruit

a basement

vegetables

a flat

a lift

Example

Apples, oranges and bananas are examples of this.

.............fruit.............

Questions

1   This takes you upstairs or downstairs
    when you don't want to walk.

....

2   People live in this. It is often on one floor.

....

3   You can sit outside your house on a
    sunny day and have a drink here.

....

4   Farms have fields with these in them.
    They are good for you.

....

5   The part of the house that is under
    the ground.

....

Part 2

Read the text and choose the best answer. There is one example.

Example

Peter: Hi, Zoe. How are you?

Zoe: A   Not today.

B   Not at all.

Ⓒ   Not very well.

Questions

1   Peter: What's the matter?

Zoe: A   I've got stomach-ache.

B   I had stomach-ache.

C   I got stomach-ache.

2 Peter: Are you going to the doctor's?

   Zoe: A   Yes, it's the doctor's.
          B   Yes, but not today.
          C   Yes, you can go.

3 Peter: Can I help you with your homework?

   Zoe: A   Yes, I can't help it.
          B   Yes, I can't spell it.
          C   Yes, I can't do it.

4 Peter: What homework have you got?

   Zoe: A   Only English.
          B   That's English.
          C   The English.

5 Peter: OK, where's your book?

   Zoe: A   But it is.
          B   Here it is.
          C   Yes it is.

6 Peter: Oh! This looks easy!

   Zoe: A   No, it wasn't!
          B   No, it doesn't!
          C   No, it hasn't!

Part 3

- 6 questions -

Read the story. Choose a word from the box. Write the correct word next to numbers 1–5. There is one example.

Last Saturday I went shopping with my friend Lily. We caught the

bus and it went slowly along the road into ....town......... . We

walked from the bus stop to the shopping centre. I bought a poster

of my favourite pop star in a shop there. His **(1)** ....

is brilliant! Then Lily wanted a T shirt to wear at the weekend, so

we went to a clothes shop and found a nice one. It had a monkey's

(2) .... on it. I found a plant for Mum at another shop,

then we caught the bus home. When I got home I showed Mum the

plant and she liked it, but then she said, 'Where's your handbag?' And

I thought, 'Oh no! It's on the bus'. We **(3)** .... to the car

and Mum drove to the **(4)** .... very quickly and found our

bus. The driver **(5)** .... at us. 'Here you are!' he said and

he gave me my handbag. I was surprised he had it, but I was really

happy too.

Example

town	face	bus station
ran	music	handbag
present	smiled	party

(6) **Now choose the best name for the story.**

Tick one box.

A terrible day ☐

A good day ☐

A quiet day ☐

Part 4

- 5 questions -

Read the text. Choose the right words and write them on the lines.

Maps

Example   Different maps ………tell……… us different things. A map

of the world can teach us about different places. From maps,

we can see the shape of different countries. A road map

on an app can show us how to go from one place to another.

1   …………………… also shows the towns and villages where

people live. You can see where the buildings are

2   …………………… a town and where the mountains are in

the countryside. Lakes and rivers are coloured blue and

3   …………………… you see green on a map, you can find

forests. Then you can learn to draw maps. They can tell

4   your friends …………………… your house is. Or you could

5   hide …………………… in the house or garden and make

a treasure map. Maps can be very exciting!

Example	tell	telling	told
1	He	It	They
2	in	on	next
3	why	which	when
4	how	where	what
5	sometimes	something	nothing

Part 5

- 7 questions -

Look at the pictures and read the story. Write some words to complete the sentences about the story. You can use 1, 2 or 3 words.

The new house

My name's Jack and I live with my Mum and Dad, and my younger sister, Daisy. She's five. Last week we moved to a new house. Dad said, 'It's got a huge garden. It's really nice. I can put a net up and you can practise scoring goals!' Daisy was really excited and danced around the living room. But I didn't want to go because my best friend lived in the house next to ours.

Examples

Jack's sister, Daisy, is .... _five_ .... years old.

Dad liked ..... _the garden_ ..... at the new house.

Questions

1   Jack's sister danced around because she was very ....

2   Jack liked living next to his .... and he wasn't happy.

Last Saturday a big truck came to our house. Two men put all my toys and comics into three boxes and took them to the truck. They dropped my laptop! They had sandwiches, talked and laughed and then they closed the doors of the truck. Then there was nothing in our house. I was sad and Daisy cried but I didn't.

3   The men carried Jack's things to the truck in ....

4   Jack's sister .... when all their things were in the truck.

Dad drove us to our new house. It was a huge house in the countryside. Mum went inside and shouted, 'Jack, come and see your new bedroom.' I ran upstairs. My room was at the top of the house. I looked out of the window and saw a field with sheep and cows in it. Then I looked at the house next to ours. It had a swimming pool and there was a boy swimming there. He waved and I thought, 'That's my new friend! Brilliant!'

5   Jack .... to see his new bedroom.

6   Jack looked out of his bedroom window, which was .... of the house.

7   In the house next to his, Jack could see a boy in ....

Part 6

- 6 questions -

Look and read and write.

Examples

The boy who is wearing black trousers is   ....skipping......

How many boys are playing football?   ....five.........

Complete the sentences.

1   The girls who are talking are sitting under   ....

2   The girl in the yellow T shirt is   ....

Answer the questions.

3   How many boys are playing tennis?   ....

4   What is the woman wearing?   ....

Now write two sentences about the picture.

5   ....

6   ....

Speaking
Find the Difference

Picture Story: Tom plays football again

Tom

Movers Vocabulary List

Students at this level are also expected to be familiar with all the words in the YLE Starters Vocabulary List which can be found in the Cambridge YLE Tests handbook.

n = noun   **v** = verb   **adj** = adjective   **prep** = preposition
num = number   **det** = determiner **adv** = adverb   **conj** = conjunction
pron = pronoun   **int** = interrogative **dis** = discourse marker **inter** = interjection
excl = exclamation

A

about **prep**
above **prep**
address **n**
afraid **adj**
after **prep**
age **n**
all **adj + pron + det**
all right **int**
along **prep**
a lot **adv**
a lot of **det**
always **adv**
another **adj**
any **adj + det**
apartment **n** (flat)
app **n**
around **prep**
asleep **adj**
aunt **n**
awake **adj**

B

back **n**
bad **adj**
badly **adv**
balcony **n**
basement **n**
bat **n**
be called **v**
bear **n**
beard **n**
because **conj**
before **adv + prep**
below **prep**
best **adj**
better **adj**
blanket **n**
blond(e) **adj**

blue **adj**
board **n**
boat **n**
body **n**
book **n**
bookcase **n**
boring **adj**
both **det + pron**
bottle (of) **n**
bottom **n**
bounce **v**
bowl (of) **n**
box **n**
boy **n**
brave **adj**
bread **n**
breakfast **n**
brilliant **adj + excl**
bring **v**
brother **n**
brown **adj**
build **v**
building **n**
burger **n**
bus **n**
bus station **n**
but **conj**
buy **v**
by **prep**
bye (-bye)

C

café **n**
car park **n**
careful(ly) **adj (adv)**
carry **v**
catch (a bus) **v**
CD **n**
cheese **n**

choose **v**
cinema **n**
circus **n**
city **n**
Clare **n**
climb **v**
cloud **n**
cloudy **adj**
clown **n**
coat **n**
coffee **n**
cold **adj + n**
come **v**
comic **n** (USA comic book)
cook **n + v**
cough **n**
country(side) **n**
cousin **n**
cry **v**
cup (of) **n**
curly **adj**

D

Daisy **n**
dance **v**
dangerous **adj**
dentist **n**
daughter **n**
difference **n**
different **adj**
difficult **adj**
doctor **n**
dolphin **n**
down **adv + prep**
downstairs **adj**
dream **n + v**
driver **n**
drop **v**

E

earache **n**
easy **adj**
e-book **n**
eighteen **num**
eighth **adj**
eleven **num**
email **v**
evening **n**
every **adj + det**
exciting **adj**
excuse me **int**

F

fair **adj**
famous **adj**
farm **n**
farmer **n**
fat **adj**
feed **v**
field **n**
fifteen **num**
fifth **adj**
film **n**
film star **n**
fine **adj**
fine! **inter**
first **adj + det**
fish **v**
fix **v**
flat **n**
floor (ground, 1st, 2nd,
   3rd, etc.) **n**
fly **n**
forest **n**
fourteen **num**
fourth **adj**
Fred **n**
Friday **n**
fruit **n**
funfair **n**

G

get un/dressed **v**
get up **v**
glass (of) **n**
go shopping **v**
goal **n**
good morning/afternoon
evening/night
granddaughter n

grandparent **n**
grandson **n**
grass **n**
great! **inter**
ground **n + adj** (floor)
grow **v**
grown up **n**

H

have (got) to **v**
have (a shower/wash) **v**
headache **n**
helmet **n**
help **v**
hide **v**
holiday **n**
home **n**
homework **n**
hop **v**
hospital **n**
hot **adj**
how **adv + int**
how about **int**
how much **adv + int**
how often **adv + int**
huge **adj**
hungry **adj**
hurt **v** (My leg hurts.
   I hurt my leg)

I

ice **n**
ice skates **n**
ice skating **n**
idea **n**
ill **adj**
in **prep of time**
inside **prep + adv**
island **n**

J

Jane **n**
Jill **n**
Jim **n**
John **n**
jungle **n**

K

kangaroo **n**
kick **n**

kind (type) **n**
kitten **n**

L

lake **n**
laptop **n**
last **adj + adv**
laugh **v**
leaf/leaves **n**
library **n**
lift **n** (USA elevator)
lion **n**
little **adj**
look for **v**
lose **v**
a lot **det + adv**
loud(ly) **adj (adv)**

M

map **n**
market **n**
Mary **n**
matter **n** (What's the
   matter?)
mean **v**
milkshake **n**
mine **pron**
mistake **n**
model **n**
Monday **n**
moon **n**
more **adj + adv**
morning **n**
most **adj + adv**
mountain **n**
moustache **n**
move **v**
music **n**
must/must not/mustn't **v**

N

naughty **adj**
near **adj + prep**
neck **n**
need **v**
net **n**
never **adv**
nineteen **num**
ninth **adj**
noodles **n**

nothing **pron**
nurse **n**

O

o'clock **adv**
off **adv**
often **adv**
on **adv**
on **prep of time**
one **pron**
only **adv**
opposite **prep**
ours **pron**
out **adv**
out of **prep**
outside **adv + prep**

P

pancake **n**
panda **n**
parent **n**
park **n**
parrot **n**
party **n**
pasta **n**
Paul **n**
penguin **n**
person/people **n**
pet **n**
Peter **n**
picnic **n**
pirate **n**
place **n**
plant **n**
playground **n**
pop star **n**
practise **v**
present **n**
puppy **n**
put on **v**

Q

quick(ly) **adj (adv)**
quiet(ly) **adj (adv)**

R

rabbit **n**
rain **n + v**
rainbow **n**
river **n**

road **n**
rock **n**
roller skating **n**
round **adj**

S

sail **v**
salad **n**
Sally **n**
sandwich **n**
Saturday **n**
sauce **n**
scarf **n**
score **v**
second **adj**
send **v**
seventeen **num**
seventh **adj**
shall **v**
shape **n**
shark **n**
shop **n + v**
shopping **n**
shoulder **n**
shout **v**
shower **n**
(have a shower) **v**
sick **adj**
sixteen **num**
sixth **adj**
skate **n + v**
skip **v**
sky **n**
slow(ly) **adj (adv)**
snail **n**
snow **n + v**
something **pron**
sometimes **adv**
son **n**
soup **n**
sports centre **n**
square **adj + n**
stair(s) **n**
star **n**
stomach **n**
straight **adj**
strong **adj**
Sunday **n**
sunny **adj**
supermarket **n**

surprised **adj**
sweater **n**
swim **n + v**
swimming pool **n**
swimsuit **n**

T

take **v**
take a bus **v**
take pictures **v**
take off **v** (get
   undressed)
tall **adj**
tea **n**
teach **v**
temperature **n**
tenth **num**
terrible **adj**
text **n**
than **conj**
theirs **pron**
then **conj + adv**
thin **adj**
thing **n**
think **n**
third **adj**
thirsty **adj**
thirteen **num**
Thursday **n**
ticket **n**
tired **adj**
tooth/teeth **n**
toothache **n**
toothbrush **n**
toothpaste **n**
top **n**
towel **n**
town **n**
tractor **n**
treasure **n**
Tuesday **n**
twelve **num**
twenty **num**

U

uncle **n**
up **adv + prep**
upstairs **adv**

V

video **n**
village **n**

W

wait **v**
wake (up) **v**
walk **n**
wash **n + v**
water **v**
waterfall **n**
wave **n**
weak **adj**
weather **n**
Wednesday **n**
week **n**
weekend **n**
well **adj + adv**
wet **adj**
whale **n**
what about **int**
what's the matter? **int**
when **adv**
which **pron**
why **int**
wind **n**
windy **adj**

work **n + v**
world **n**
worse **adj**
worst **adj**
would/n't (like) **v**
wrong **adj**

X

(no words at this level)

Y

yesterday **n + adj**
yours **pron**

Z

Zoe **n**
zoo **n**